CONNEMARA TWILIGHT
(and other scrivenings)

Emily McCormack

1663 Liberty Drive, Suite 200
Bloomington, Indiana 47403
(800) 839-8640
www.AuthorHouse.com

© *2006 Emily McCormack. All Rights Reserved.*

No part of this book may be reproduced, stored in a retrieval system, or transmitted by any means without the written permission of the author.

First published by AuthorHouse 01/26/05

ISBN: 1-4259-0789-X (sc)

Library of Congress Control Number: 2005910749

Printed in the United States of America
Bloomington, Indiana

This book is printed on acid-free paper.

Picture (Connemara, at Dusk) reproduced with permission of Liam Blake

Also by the Author

Fourteen Points

Temporary Assignments, B.C.*
(*Before Computers)

Mostly About Books

Never a Teardrop

Dedicated to the memory of

Jerry Voorhis

(a.k.a. Jerry O'Voorhis,
Honorary Irishman)

TABLE OF CONTENTS

CONNEMARA TWILIGHT 1
SOMEWHERE REVISITED 2
REMEMBERING CORDELIA 4
LUDWIG van BEETHOVEN (1770-1827) 6
REFLECTIONS ON WORDSWORTH'S RECOLLECTIONS .. 7
TRANSUBSTANTIATION 8
DESPAIR 9
NOCTURNE 10
SEPTEMBER 11
ON FIRST LOOKING INTO "ON FIRST LOOKING INTO". 12
REFRACT IONS 13
SUBJUNCTIVE MOOD 14
OF ONE SUBSTANCE 15
CHRISTMAS, 1972 16
A SHORT COURSE IN PHILOSOPHY 17
THE LADDER 19
NO PAROLE 20
ERGO EGO 21
BREEZES 22
AGE OF LIGHT -- AND DARK 23
STOLEN FROM SHAKESPEARE 25
OWED TO QWERTY 26
THE REAL LIFE 27
MILTON'S PARADISE FOUND 28
CONSIDERATIONS 29
GENESIS: Epilogue 30

LAKE MICHIGAN	31
OGDEN NASH -- A REALIO, TRULIO POET	32
CONSULTATIVE MANAGEMENT	33
THE SPY WHO CAME IN FROM THE COLD WAR	34
IN GRATITUDE	35
PUNCTUATION PROFILED	36
EASE	38
THE LEPERS	39
I THOUGHT I FORGOT YOU	40
TO THOMAS MOORE AT AVOCA	41
CONFRONTED WITH GOODNESS	42
STYLE SHOW	43
REVIEWING THE REVIEWS	44
THE LONG AGO FEELING	45
SEASONAL LOVE	46
NEVER A TEARDROP	47
LOVE REMEMBERED	48
JOURNEY	49
TIME	50
A NORMANDY SONNET	51
DO NOT DISTURB	52
SECOND THOUGHTS	54
EYE RHYMES	55
TURN BACK THE WORLD	56
DON'T VACUUM DURING WAGNER	57
AUTHOR? AUTHOR?	59
THEIR GLORY EXCEEDS	60
ANDANTE	61
DEAREST EMILY --	62

CONNEMARA TWILIGHT

When twilight comes to Connemara
And covers ev'ry hedge and stone,
It bathes the land in windswept beauty
Long borrowed from a world unknown.

When twilight comes to Connemara,
It falls on lake and rock and bluff.
While I behold the landscape, spellbound,
It seems like heaven in the rough.

> This rugged corner in west Erin
> Will never, never set me free,
> For here it is I have my being --
> A happy, willing slavery.

When twilight comes to Connemara,
Then I remember someone who
Once kissed me gently and caressed me
And wept while whispering *adieu*.

SOMEWHERE REVISITED

Sometimes when we're least aware

A strange thing comes to be:

We hear a distant echo

From buried memory.

      Anything can strike the chord --

      Both commonplace and rare --

      The sight of southbound swallow --

      The scent of snow-tinged air --

      Seeing hearthfire red ablaze --

      Or azure summer sky --

      Hearing rousing tavern song --

      Or *lieder* lullaby.

And then within a heartbeat

We sight familiar shore,

With half-remembered feeling

That we've been here before.

      It's over in an instant

      If reckoned in our time.

      (Such moments must be measured

By far and diff'rent clime.)

We pause, still filled with wonder

At this elusive toll

Evoking in our being

Nostalgia of the soul.

REMEMBERING CORDELIA

Prometheus, I light a brighter sky
   With fire, stolen yet again.
Fair Plato, the bubble of your dream
   I prick to find reality.
O, tongue-tied Cicero, lay down your scroll
   And let me speak for you.
Bold Alexander, weep, weep afresh.
   I 've conquered all the world.
Hurry back to Corinth, Paul,
   And hide the prize. My foot is fleet.
Cortez, your seamen, you, and Darien,
   I reduce to but a speck in my expanding universe.
Giaconda, yes, I understand your smile.
   There never was a mystery.
Dear Robert, grow old without me, all alone.
   The wax of my eloquence outshines your words.
And Beethoven, I lead a deaf'ning blast
   Before an orchestra subdued.

Sweet William, when you arrive at Innisfree,

    You'll find that I'd been there -- and fled.

Sigmund, even with your many moods,

    You'll never plumb the chambers of my heart.

But <u>you</u>! You ask to hear my love.

    I stand before you: bowed -- humbled -- awed. Mute.

LUDWIG van BEETHOVEN (1770-1827)

I heard you again last night
And listened as you told me,
One more time, of all that you knew.

I love the way you call me,
Your gentle *pianos* whispering,
Your *fortes* insisting,
Repeating, repeating, repeating,
To be sure I understand.

I hear, too, your brave silences,
Your never-ending *codas*,
Your triumphant *finales*
That, for me, are just the beginning.

As I travel toward you,
Beyond time, beyond space,
We meet at last, and I hear again
Your invitation:
                    ....Listen, listen with me.

REFLECTIONS ON WORDSWORTH'S RECOLLECTIONS

Where were we in that other then
That somehow 'scapes our present ken?

Why is it we can't quite recall
The other life, the other thrall?

This prisonhouse looms large, and yet,
The former manse we can't forget.

Lonely for our clouds of glory,
We find this moment desultory.

As children, inarticulate,
We little understood our fate.

But as we travel from our Star,
Equipped with words, we know how far.

Our loss, alas, well we measure,
As we recount the one-time treasure.

What finger etched in us this yearning
And beckons us to be returning?

Where were we in that other then?
Can we -- at last -- go back again?

TRANSUBSTANTIATION

Musings on Wilde's Reading -- Keats's Urn
        Auden's Icarus -- Moore's Avoca
The elements are there -- and the mystery --
    *   A ballad
    *   A vase
    *   A painting
    *   A place
Waiting -- wondering -- we witness --
    The influence of confluence
    The prisms of prisons
    The crash of man splashing
    The vessel in verse

        ****

Reading is the ritual --
Each of us Melchisedek --
Time -- the acolyte -- suspends --
Essence into essence blends --
    Arising -- not as admiration --
    Nor longer as appreciation --
    But art emerging as creation --
    Startling in its alteration!

        ****

DESPAIR

What soul has known those endless hours
When hoped-for tears--moist, soothing flow'rs--
Would not move?

What soul has cried out, all alone,
With heart one loud, unspoken groan,
Just for love?

Is there a soul for peace who craves,
With heart engulfed by dark'ning waves
Of deep despair?

What soul has clutched the very sod
To still the fear that even God
Would not be there?

If such a person truly be,
Don't hesitate to come to me.
I'll understand.

I'll know. For once my spirit broke.
Oh, how I longed for just the stroke
Of someone's hand.

NOCTURNE

Lovely visions of the night.
White clouds drifting.
Moon in flight.

And I gaze with sleepless eyes
Out into the
Darkened skies.

Night sounds whisper tenderly.
Gentle starlight
Covers me.

Mem'ries that I thought at rest
Stirring now
Within my breast.

Meetings. Partings. Bittersweet.
Moments perfect.
Joys complete.

I relive each dream I see.
But the spell
Ends quietly.

White clouds drifting.
Moon in flight.
Lovely visions of the night.

SEPTEMBER

September is a state of mind --
A kind of lovely madness --
When autumn hues match autumn moods,
All golden-tinged with sadness.

Eleven months ' immunity
Can't stop September's turnout.
Discarded dreams enflame again,
Glow bright, then slowly burn out.

Though rapt we are within its spell
(September symptoms hover!) --
Yet we release our hold and then
Reluctantly recover.

ON FIRST LOOKING INTO "ON FIRST LOOKING INTO"

Long have I wandered in the stores of books,
And many boring tracts and pamphlets read;
To many famous authors I've been led
By publishers with avaricious looks.
Drummed was I, and brainwashed, yes, yes, gadzooks!
On thin, worn path to library I sped.
But not till -- with finger poised, spittle-fed --
I read Keats felt I prose's gentle hooks.

At last I understood how it must seem
Whene'er a rocket, spun out, touches down;
And weightless Lindbergh, as though in a dream,
Strides out upon the moon, Earth's silver crown,
While watching TV'd folk fear they blaspheme,
Yet thrill as vicars of the great renown.

REFRACT IONS

The eye I eye in the mirror
        Eyes me back with a steady gaze.
        And the eye I see
                Seems to say to me
        That the eye I eye
                Is reality
        And the eyeing eye but a haze.

The I I eye in my mem'ry
        Eyes me back from within my mind
        And the I I know
                Knows where'er I go
        That the I I eye
                Is forever so
        For the I for aye is designed.

SUBJUNCTIVE MOOD

I could scale the heights and plumb the depths.
I could move mountains and grow roses in the sand.
I could chart galaxies, slow constellations,
    Change the course of the universe.

Then when I spoke, angel-tongued,
My words would crash and resound -- not tinkle --
And the world would listen.

    All this could I do -- and more! --
    If only you loved me.

OF ONE SUBSTANCE

Some where, some place
Between night and light
There is a flash of space,
An inch of time,
Suspended -- poised --
Waiting to be.

It is then, it is there,
As if a door, shut tight,
Is suddenly opened,
Releasing a myriad of thoughts,
feelings, sensations.

And they come tumbling into your being,
Riotously, wantonly, unchecked, and alive!
Quickly you must put them into their
proper places,
Separating them into their pigeonholes
Of past, future, maybe, and never.

Just as you become aware of what
you are about,
It is all over,
And there you are -- *now!*

CHRISTMAS, 1972

Angel, mute your Christmas lay.
A soldier's dying far away.

Shine, O Star, with gentle light
Upon a refugee in flight.

Christmas bell, subdue your chime.
We can't rejoice this Christmastime.

Shepherd, you were first to know.
Help us find the path to go.

Wise Man, tell us what you heard
And comfort us. You saw the Word.

You Who came to share our grief:
Tiny Child, restore belief.

A SHORT COURSE IN PHILOSOPHY

Dear Socrates with shrewish wife
Spent all his time defining life.
But Plato said it is a dream
And things are just not what they seem.
Comes now Tom with holy bottle:
"Let me baptize Aristotle."

Rene, drunk, ergo'd Cartesian:
"Thinking, am-ing ish the reashon."
Shaky Willie, the all-seeing,
Asking: "Being or non-being?"
Turn to Wordsworth if you're fretting:
"Just remember: we're forgetting."

If, in taking up the long view,
Must we sacrifice our fun, too?

Omar Khay says: "Drink, be merry.
Pretty soon they you will bury."
Jean-Paul Sartre, with accent nasal:
"Living? Why, it's only basal."
T.S. left us wasting, hanging:
"Whimper, folks! You're sure not banging."

Whoe'er started all this business --
Quiddity and thought and is-ness?
Heady knowledge, *a priori*,
Very, very hard to live by.

Rave on, thinker, writer, poet!
This life's over 'fore you know it.
Frankly, Scarlett's words let's borrow:
Damn the worry till tomorrow.

THE LADDER

Time ticks gently when we're young.
Days of frolic. Songs are sung.
Visions bright and hopes far-flung
On life's lowest ladder-rung.

Soon we start our steady climb,
Suddenly aware of time
Beating its insistent rhyme,
Marked by lonely, wistful chime.

Footsteps falter, breath agasp.
Ladder's midpoint in our clasp.
Feeling splintered years' rough rasp.
Moments slipping from our grasp.

We continue our ascent
Up the ladder, passions spent,
Wond'ring where the hours went,
What it all has really meant.

Reaching top where time is through,
Strange horizon within view.
Ladder's last rung leads us to
Unknown world. We start anew.

NO PAROLE

Time is my jailer
And space is my cell.
My crime was to be
My sentence as well.

ERGO EGO

It never caused me much remorse
To put Descartes before Deshorse.

Though Socrates can make you think,
I wouldn't recommend his drink.

Old Aristotle, he who gave
Six basic plots, says one's the grave.

Tom of Aquin's words and rhymes
Proved God is living seven times.

To Persia's Omar listen up:
He'll slice your bread and fill your cup.

A dream, says Plato. How absurd!
When nightmare is the proper word.

We are existing, opines Sartre.
Not much at best. But it's a start.

BREEZES

This fleeting moment I will seize
To sing the praises of the breeze.

The breeze is like a dear friend who
Will, unexpected, visit you.

The unassuming little breeze
Has blessed the world for centuries.

I'd rather have a good breeze than
A noisy old electric fan.

A breeze cools more than just your skin.
It also cools the you within.

The heat of day it helps erase
And hints about a better place.

Next time we're down upon our knees
Let's whisper thank you for the breeze.

AGE OF LIGHT -- AND DARK

Of past events inscibed below in numbers five times three,
Some are light and some are dark---and all called history.

    "He came. He saw. He conquered all
    And sent reports back home."
    Thus fell the great declensions
    When Gibbon spoke of Rome.

    In France we see the Sansculottes
    And peasants sans their bread.
    Worthy Burke, he might as well
    Have left his word unsaid.
    Who crowns himself? A Corsican?
    The world is on its knees.
    Ill-clad soldiers marching off
    To serve -- to starve -- to freeze.

    When he awoke he found the Don
    Had brought him lasting fame.
    Luddites smashed machinery.
    A ship bore Fulton's name.
    A monster born of gentle hand
    As black men break the sod.
    Heroic man going deaf,
    He shakes his fist at God.

A Spaniard dates the third of May.
America sets sale.
Hegel writes his treatises.
The blind can see with Braille.

We read of all they have to tell and wonder what they'll say,
Those writers of tomorrow, when studying today.

STOLEN FROM SHAKESPEARE

Infant, vaguely seeing form,
Drowsy, helpless, loved and warm.

Tiny child discovers earth
Mingled with his private mirth.

Growing boy self-consciously
Groping for identity.

Young man filled with bursting heart,
Over threshold makes his start.

Hardly have his dreams begun,
Middle age o'ertakes each one.

Failing sight and trembling hands,
All alone, he understands

What must be his final goal:
Vesting for another role.

OWED TO QWERTY

Ev'ry guy and ev'ry gertie
Sings your praises, dear old QWERTY.
Off my back I'd give my shirty
For your row of keys so purty.

Often jammed, like fate so flirty,
Or when life gets down and dirty,
You spring up with vengeance spurty --
Steadfast, stalwart, straight and sturdy.

All the other keys so wordy
Next to you seem crass and nerdy.
With one hand I hail you, QWERTY!
My shift's over. Off to
XXX

THE REAL LIFE

Of all the many lives we lead
While roaming far and wide,
We know there's only one *that's* real:
The life we live inside.

We build our treasured monuments
And point to them with pride.
But all the while we know what's real:
The life we live inside.

Again we search throughout the world,
Where good and bad abide,
To learn once more what's only real:
The life we live inside.

It make no difference what we seem
Or matter what we hide.
We can't escape the one thing real:
The life we live inside.

MILTON'S PARADISE FOUND

Tell me not with arms akimbo
That there is a hell or limbo.
Paradise is what I'm seeking,
And I know that God is peeking.

I must have my inspiration
At the start of the creation
With birds and beasts and sunlight clear
And ev'rything so brand-new here.

See that handsome couple frolic,
Jaybird-naked, young, bucolic.
I'll approach them, call them hither,
Caution them of fateful slither:

"Don't go near that tree this a.m.
It will only lead to mayhem."
They listened not to my words terse,
So now I get to write my verse.

CONSIDERATIONS

'Tis said that music, art, and rhyme
Reflect each period of time.

The open book, the written word
Can help to teach what has occurred.

If we would know what lies ahead,
We first must study days long dead.

The bygone fate contains the hint
Of lasting humankind's imprint.

What's happened to the landscape bright
Which Wordsworth wrote of with delight?

Is this the wasteland here we see
That Eliot proclaimed would be?

We have replaced Walt Whitman's song
With whimper, wearisome and long.

"Time's out of joint." Oh, Hamlet, your
Utterance was premature.

Now at roadfork, trembling, we
Ourselves will shape our destiny.

GENESIS: Epilogue

Light and life and matter.
Indestructibility.

Soil and sea and heavens.
Ineluctability.

Bird and beast and Adam.
                    Autocreativity.

LAKE MICHIGAN

Restless -- restless -- one of five --
Languid -- lapping -- leaping -- <u>live</u> --

Sprawling southward -- stretching north --
Lovely shoreline calling forth --

Winter-frozen -- summer-warm --
Springtime-thawing -- autumn-storm --

Waves-amountain -- rocks adash --
Slow to settle -- quick to lash --

Waters sparkling with allure --
Onetime-pristine -- made impure --

Calm in moonlight -- wild at day --
Girds for battle -- foes at bay --

Wounded -- raging -- full-awake --
Reigns at last -- -- triumphant Lake!

OGDEN NASH -- A REALIO, TRULIO POET

There once was a promising lad
Who said: "I'll write poetry bad."
Yes, his rhymes were absurd,
But he stuck to his word,
And he stretched things out here and there
Once in a while every so often just a tad.

CONSULTATIVE MANAGEMENT

What's happened to the good old days
When I used to be boss,
With full responsibility
For profit and for loss?

I'd say to my employees then:
"Do this!" And it was done.
I really kept them on the go
And had them on the run.

But times have changed, and methods, too.
Alas and oh alack!
We cannot do a doggone thing
Until we yak and yak.
It's even hit my home, this trend,
And things are on the skids.
Before I make a single move,
I've got to ask the kids.

Yet after all, I should not moan,
For there is much to praise.
I heard a rumor just today:
My staff gave me a raise.

THE SPY WHO CAME IN FROM THE COLD WAR

The dagger's sheathed and rusty.
The cloak is tattered, worn.
The microfilm is full exposed.
The cipher book is torn
No more a secret rendezvous
Or meeting near the lake.
No switching satchels at the train
Or hidden pix to take.

"Oh, those were days of glory,"
He whispers with a sigh,
And ponders deep within his heart:
"Oh, CIA, oh why?"

IN GRATITUDE

I saw Cortez at Darien.
I felt a coward's kiss.
I roamed afar with Homer
Was thrilled by Wordsworth's bliss.

I visited a wasteland
I dropped a tear with Boz.
I walked a mile at Walden
And even danced at Oz.

I triumphed at Thermopylae.
The darkness I espied.
I numbered gulags by the score.
With hosts of heroes died.

I plucked a flower at Flanders.
Wept when a mother chose.
I travelled to the Courthouse.
I rearranged my foes.

All this within a lifetime,
These gifts of word and deed.
With bursting heart I breathe my thanks:
Oh God! I love to read!

PUNCTUATION PROFILED
(Parentheses)

Curved little twins
With their scholarly stoop.
    Psychologically Siamese.
    Humble, officially unnecessary.
Yet embracing truth --
Fragmented, afloat flotsam-like
On a sea of words --
    Waiting to be uttered by
    By some hoarse Hamlet
    In a searing aside.

    Comma,
Common, common comma,
Misused and abused,
Ingratiating, groveling, Glick-like,
And too, too available.

    Colon :
Inflexible column standing at attention
Preparing to pontificate
ex Cathedra pronouncements: : : : : :

    Period.
Dogmatic dot!
As though speculation
Ceases with a
Speck in space.

Question ? Mark
Ancient and arthritic
Bent and burdened
With the ageless WHY?
Favorite of philosophers and fools.

EASE

I think that I shall always try
To sit around and versify.
The hours are good and so's the pay.
Plus, I can sleep till noon each day.

Reg'lar toil's for other jerks.
But not for me. I need my perks.
If Shakespeare, Browning, Omar Khay
Achieved great fame, then why can't I?

I'll moon and June among the best,
And also, I won't lose my rest.
Only one thing bothers me:
Who in hell will plant that tree?

THE LEPERS

They traveled all together
And numbered half a score.
"Unclean! Unclean! Unclean!" they cried
With tinkling bell before.

Then Someone heard them calling
And begging for His cure.
He sent them off rejoicing,
Complete and free and pure.

When one returned much later
To give a grateful sign,
The Healer asked him sadly:
"Where are the other nine?"

I THOUGHT I FORGOT YOU

I thought I forgot you.
Then I heard the rain,
And suddenly there
You were with me again.

I thought I forgot you.
But I touched a rose
And watched in the moonlight
As you lay in repose.

    You come back in fragments
    In summer and fall,
    In winter and springtime --
    And night, most of all.

I thought I forgot you.
Then I saw the snow,
And now I remember:
I still love you so.

TO THOMAS MOORE AT AVOCA

Stared you at this rock, oh Tom?
Heard that lapping sound?
Was your sky an azure, too,
As you gazed around?

Everything and nothing's changed
Since you wrote your word.
Miles and miles the waters flowed.
Many hearts have stirred.

Divider Time does not rule here.
A gentler hand holds sway.
The waters keep their rendezvous,
And I met you today.

A valley calls each one of us
To share amid our friends
And find at last that blessed peace
Where mem' ry never ends.

CONFRONTED WITH GOODNESS

Sweetness I had known --
Geoffrey's April and William's Adversity.

And Love. Much of that.
Ben. Byron and Bysshe. Robert/Elizabeth.
Yes, even Keats's Half-love.

Schiller showed me Joy.
For Courage I had Babington.
Pride I learned from Cullen and Stephen.
From Jonathan -- Truth.

For Philosophy I had Plato.
Thomas guided me to Independence.

I thought myself well prepared.

Wrong as I. For I met you.
And you confronted me with your goodness.
Confronted and disarmed me.

Then you left me. Bared of soul. Alone.
Humbled. Ennobled. Exalted.

STYLE SHOW

It wasn't much -- a rag of a day in November.
But you wore it well and gave it style.

Then came December, ermined.
You matched its elegance.

January was shopworn.
But somehow you managed to make its shabbiness genteel.

    And so the months covered you, one by one,
    Dark or bright, according to their moods.

But, oh, June! How it became you.
Its brilliance captured yours.

Yes. In June you dazzled me.

REVIEWING THE REVIEWS

Go fetch me the Thesaurus,
And bring me Webster's, too.
Then let us lay before us
The critic's new review.

I think it is absurd, luv,
The language that's employed.
Some words I've never heard of
Like "Zeitgeist" and "sangfroid."

Now I find Brahms a poet,
And Beethoven is keen.
But "Last night's Bach -- inchoate."
Whatever does that mean?

When writing of a movie,
A book, a play, a waltz,
What's wrong with words like "groovy,"
"Not bad," or just plain "schmaltz"?

Please, critics, not so classy,
Though you must have your fun.
I'm begging you, en masse-y,
For syllables of one.

THE LONG AGO FEELING

I've got that long ago feeling,
That lonely long ago feeling.
Those days of friendship and giving
And day-to-day living
That come back to haunt you --
Oh, where have they gone to?

I've got that long ago feeling,
That longing long ago feeling.
Those nights of music and laughter
And happily after
That slipped through our fingers --
Their loveliness lingers.

So long ago, long ago, long, long, long ago.

SEASONAL LOVE

When words of love I wish to utter --
My heart aflipping and aflutter --
I start to stammer and to stutter.
The more I try, the more I mutter.

It happens ev'ry springtime season
While watching flow'rs with all their bees on:
I find no proper prose to seize on.
There's little logic, rhyme or reason.

In summertime it is the same --
When, like the sun, my heart's aflame.
I find excuses, each one lame,
With no one but myself to blame.

At autumntime with colors golden
The words at last should me embolden.
But now my tongue in cotton's rolled in.
And ev'ry syllable I hold in.

Ah winter! Such a time of bliss.
My final chance. I cannot miss.
So to my love I'll say but this:
"Too cold to talk. Why not just kiss."

NEVER A TEARDROP

If things will go according to my plan,
The roses that you touch will have no thorn.
The clouds above you will be silver-lined,
And you'll awake to happiness each morn.

    Never a teardrop.
    Never a heartache.
    That's all I ask for you.

    Sunshine and laughter.
    Happiness after.
    Friendships both old and new.

In all my planning -- in all my dreaming --
In all my prayers for you -- there is

    Never a teardrop.
    Never a heartache.
    Nothing but love for you.

LOVE REMEMBERED

Trembling close to sweet surrender --
Chaste embrace and kiss so tender --
Love unfurled in all its splendor.

But searing in my memory,
I knew somehow it could not be,
For you were never meant for me.

It was over, hardly started.
You and love have both departed,
I remain here, broken-hearted.

This is the price that I must pay.
But I'll remember come what may:
You brought me love for one brief day.

JOURNEY

When our sunny mornings
Quicken into noon
And our glance is skyward,
There we find the moon.

All our brief forevers --
Ev'ry day and night --
Gathering momentum,
Suddenly take flight.

Each of us alone now,
Stript of time and space,
As we journey on, to
Seek another place.

TIME

"When" is a place
Somewhere in space
That we cannot trace.

We should not care
To go back "where."
We can't return there.

    Thus we proceed --
    Sun in the lead --
    Incredible speed.

        If we but strive,
        Shall we arrive
        To find Now alive?

A NORMANDY SONNET

What are those pinpoints on the yellowed maps?
Can we not leave the scroll of war uncurled?
Must we smell blood and see young bodies hurled?
We ask: Was this worth fighting for? Perhaps.
The dates, the times, the places...mem' ries lapse...
For there is much distracting in this world.
We hear the drums, we see the flags unfurled.
A bent old man salutes when he hears taps.

Forgetful time our crosses soon will bleach
Beneath the sun and wind and hail and rain.
Who will the younger generation teach
About our grief, our fear, our loss, our pain?
With our stilled voices not within their reach,
They must remember: This was not in vain.

Written June 6, 1994
The 50th anniversary of D-Day

DO NOT DISTURB

Something after bedtime prayer.
Something magic in the air.
Something -- nameless yet, but deep --
Comes alive while mortals sleep.
Then it is that odes are born.
Never at the break of morn.
Never in the high of noon.
But always by the light of moon.

Not a rhyme or roundelay
Was e'er writ by light of day.
As the other folk lie dreaming,
Poets do their scanning, scheming.
Anything to do with <u>matin</u>
Is strictly for the scholar Latin.
While the poets' minds are soaring
Usually their mates are snoring.

At Dawning. Every single line
Was written during lunar shine.
Why think you Milton lost his sight?
From doing all his work at night.
Hamlet, Home, Trees, and *Skylark.*
These are products of the dark.
Shelley, Shakespeare, Edgar Guest
Didn't get their proper rest.

Many poems are generic.
Others you will find Homeric.
Some poets, geniuses -- some, hacks.
But all of them: insomniacs.
In the New Life, by and by,
At that sweet Dorm in the sky --
Pass the gate with tiptoed shoes.
Bards at last will have their snooze.

SECOND THOUGHTS

Sir, I do not like your views.
                Your views I do not care to choose.
                Your views, I find, do not amuse.

Miss, I surely like your smile.
                Your smile is sweet and full of guile.
                Your smile, I find, is just my style.

Sir, my mind has had a change.
                A change most sudden and quite strange.
                A change, I find, I can arrange.

EYE RHYMES

Unfortunate
About your fate

You were unknown
In this small town

However, now
You are laid low

We should have seen
What you had been

No gal alive
Can quite forgive

What you have done
We cast a stone

At females slight
Who wear size eight

TURN BACK THE WORLD

Turn back the world to that place --
To that place where our dreams all came true --
To that night when you said, "I love you."
Turn it back. Turn it back. Please do.

Turn back the world to that time --
When our songs made our cares disappear --
When our laughter rang out sweet and clear.
Turn it back. Turn it back, my dear.

> Though our happiness spun off its course,
> Let's retrace ev'ry smile, ev'ry kiss.
> We can set our direction again
> To recapture those moments of bliss.

Turn back the world once again.
Turn it back and hold on to it fast.
Make our future become what was past.
Maybe this time we can make it last.

DON'T VACUUM DURING WAGNER

You may mop during Mozart if you must.
And if Debussey's played, then you may dust.
You may bake during Bach,
      during jazz,
      during rock,
But when Wagner is playing, please be shushed!!!

Don't Vacuum during Wagner, I implore.
When Chopin's being played, then do your chore.

When Tristan sings of love
With th'Evening Star above,
Don't Vacuum during Wagner, I implore.

Don't Vacuum during Wagner or I'll weep.
When Strauss is being strummed, then you may sweep.

When Elsa dreams her dream,
Or at Flying Dutchman's theme,
Don't Vacuum during Wagner or I'll weep.

      Some music is so pleasing to the ear,
      All other sound should cease!!!
      So we can hear.

Don't Vacuum during Wagner, I insist.
I don't care what you're doing during Liszt.

When Walter's song is sung,
Or at Gotterdammerung
      Don't Vacuum during Wagner!
      Don't Vacuum during Wagner!
Don't Vacuum during Wagner, I insist.

AUTHOR? AUTHOR?

If all the world's a stage,
And if the play's the thing,
We strutters, stars, and actors
Demand a rewriting.

THEIR GLORY EXCEEDS

Unimagined galaxies
With miles in shorthand light
    The blackened sky
    Attracts my eye
    A cowboy's word
    Again is heard
    And I must scan
    My vision's span
Of panoramic night
The restless moon foregrounded
Flirting and amoral
    Chased and chasing
    Clouds embracing
    In coquette style
    Distracts a while
    Appears Recedes
    Abruptly speeds
As from a lovers' quarrel
Singling out a lonely star
To contemplate its worth
    The mystery
    Eluding me
    While I would know
    What makes it glow
    A cry of pain
    Divides my train
And pulls me back to earth

ANDANTE

Slow, oh slow. Please tell me slow.
Recall once more lost yesterdays.
Lull me with their memories
Sun-streaked. Endless love's delays.

Wait, oh wait. Postpone your leave.
Keats' nightingale with us remains.
Stay, the fleeting moment clasped.
Ecstasy so shortly reigns.

Soon, too soon, the harsh discord
Intrudes with an insistent rush.
And stern finale's crash demands
A total silence -- not a hush.

DEAREST EMILY --

Your gentle presence in our midst
At last we understand.
We searched for style and found the dash
The rhyme -- the glovéd hand.

The crystal beauty of your words
Shines forth throughout the years.
Your fragmented reality
Is music to our ears.

Now you can settle in your tomb --
For seniors, middle, youth --
We listen, as you tell us (slant):
The truth is still the truth.

Printed in the United States
44886LVS00006B/232-249